Come To The Garden

Sheila Nielsen

BookLeaf Publishing

India | USA | UK

Made with ❤ on the BookLeaf Publishing Platform
www.bookleafpub.in
www.bookleafpub.com

Dedication

To those dear ones who celebrate the power of words to capture the wonder of nature. May you find peace in this beautiful world.

Preface

Words like sparkles and sprinkles
often found on solitary walks
hidden under blossoms and leaves
flitting about like delicate butterflies
serving as my source of inspiration

I resist the urge to force my poetry
Instead, I let it come to me slowly
as a simple idea or pleasant sensation
a delightful treasure of ideas ~
words like sparkles and sprinkles

Poetry comes to me in memories
quiet moments of reflection
in gardens and woodlands
In sunrises and sunsets ~
often found on solitary walks

I focus on the tiny elements
found in my natural surroundings
songbirds and chattering squirrels,
charming beetles and little ladybugs ~
hidden under blossoms and leaves

Even in profound adversity
nature has a way of resisting
Storms may violently rage
yet hope and ideas rise in defiance ~
flitting about like delicate butterflies

And so I write about what I see
Lifted and encouraged by life
whether in thoughts or dreams
or happy days ~ all of these
serving as my source of inspiration

Please walk with me ~ Sheila

Acknowledgements

I began writing poetry when the world was in lockdown with the pandemic. It was with the support and encouragement of my friends and family that I began to find my voice. I have written about feeling like an imposter in the poetic world. I love learning about poetic styles, forms, and rhythms, often with the intent of sharing them with my students and incorporating them into readings and assignments, but I did not see myself as a poet. Some months later, I presented a few poems at an open-mic event, and I was recognized by a young woman. We sat together waiting and talking about the weather in the lobby at the shop of a local mechanic. While we talked, she smiled and said, "I know you! You're the poet I heard at the university." In that flash, I embraced my poetry in earnest. I will continue to write for myself and those sweet ones in my heart ~ my dear husband, Michael, and our children, Kelly and Paul, and for wonderful friends, family, and students with whom I connect through shared experiences and memories. You have my deepest appreciation and love. Please enjoy this small collection.

Sheila

Swing Free

Swing into your dreams, child
hear the whisper of the clouds
calling your name

Come to me come to me come
with all your hopes and dreams
Rise high and touch the sun

Find strength as you pump and pull
higher and higher and higher
defying laws of gravity

Close your eyes and envision
all the glorious possibilities
the universe has waiting for you

Your imagination is wild and free
blowing in the gentle wind
like Dandelion wishes flying high

Return every day and swing, sweet child
dream and dream and dream again
The sky has no limits for dreamers

In the Garden

Come to the garden
a respite from the world
find a gentle peace

Rest in solitude
commune with your Creator
be free of worries

When you feel centered
ready to take on the day
assured and restored

May peace guide your steps
Go forward with confidence
in service and love

Take My Hand

Take my hand, child
lest you trip and fall.
The paths we traverse in life
are treacherous at every turn
often uncertain

Sometimes the shadows
linger in the byways and
along the old highways
So, take my hand
for assurance

Readily you reach for me
with trust and confidence
Lift your eyes to the road ahead
always stepping forward
with conviction

Oh, how our roles change
with every step we take and
every decision we make
growing in confidence
grounded and strong

Now you smile and lead
Casting away the sorrows
and embracing the joy
Take my hand, child
lest I stumble and fall.

Let Me Share Your Heart

I know I can't take away your sorrow
and nothing I say or do
can stop the cascade of tears that
flow with each memory

The testament of true love
is measured by the vacuous void
and the chasm that has been
torn in your heart

Perhaps you rationalize that
the tremendous loss you feel
is not any different from what
others have experienced for millennia

While it is true that death is
no discriminator of persons,
your loss and sorrow are unique to you
and should not be restrained

There will be many days of grief,
and anniversaries in all iterations
will carry the weight of love
remembered and love lost

Perhaps in time the memories will
offer solace and peace and the
acute pain of loss will be diminished
though never entirely forgotten

Through this process, I will remain
by your side to share your memories,
to hold your hand, and to just listen
with my ears and with my heart

Because the true measure of
our deep and abiding friendship
will never be lost in the prattle of words
but found in the quiet moments we share.

If Your Life Was a Book

If your life was a book,
would you slip through the pages
and relish each word?

Would you stop to reread the passages
and take in the tender moments,
feeling and tasting both
sweetness and sorrow in life?

Perhaps your life is a page-turner
with gripping moments of
excitement and uncertainty?

Are you living your life with
continuity lacing together
storylines and characters to
build deep personal connections?

If your life was a book,
would you want others
to read and share it?

Isn't it a wonderful idea
to consider your life as a book
in which you are both the
author and the reader?

Wouldn't it be lovely to go to the garden
to rest and read the incredible story
of the life you have chosen for yourself?

Come to the Altar

All are welcomed at the altar
Bring your sorrows and joys
Let communion begin
deep in your heart and be
whispered to the heavens

All are welcomed at the altar
because creation and salvation
are universally extended
regardless of your position,
status, orientation, or creed

All are welcomed at the altar
invited and wholly accepted
in peace and tranquility
lifting voices in unity and
harmony for all eternity

Elegy for the Trees

I sit in solitude in the cool and comforting shadows
Gazing up through branches reaching heavenward.
I mourn today as you are brutally sacrificed
for grind and gravel as industry moves forward

All around are trees hewn coarsely to the ground
Leaving behind miles of barren waste and pain
Pesticides are killing pollinators and tainting soil
While herbicides are ravaging seedlings with their stain

God, in Heaven above – were not trees and animals
the first to bless this land in glory and light?
Did not the days of creation prepare this earth
in wonderous bounty for our eternal birthright?

Is there hope in this dismal world for redemption?
Forgive us, dear Father, for this global catastrophe.
Our greed and reckless exploitation reveal our shame.
As repentant children, we bow humbly before thee.

Today, dear Father – please take our hearts and hands
Grant us wisdom to restore this beautiful earth.
Welcome back the glorious trees and birds and bees
to their sanctuary and this place of our humble birth.

No Words

I am torn with soul-wrenching sadness
A hatchling has fallen from the nest
and is struggling on the ground.
There are only two bad choices:
I can leave the foundling untouched
thus assuring certain death.

That is a stark and harsh reality.
The other choice is to try and
lift it gently and return it to the nest.
This is also a death sentence because
the adult birds will reject the tiny one
who bears the scent of humans.

Rejection will also assure its death.
I am helpless to change the outcome.
I'm heartbroken that the rules of nature
are so deeply defined that I am utterly
powerless to save a beautiful creature
whose gift is simply to sing.

Going Back to My Roots

I think in another life I
thrived on the wild frontier,
living off the land and
working under the blistering sun,
growing my own food,
and sewing my own clothes.

I was that child reading
by crackling fires tucked
into hand-made quilts
and rising early to
milk cows and gather eggs.

These shadowy recollections
entrenched in my psyche,
are part of my long heritage.

Haunting memories and dreams
are awakened in me when I see
blueberries ready to harvest
and peaches promising
a bounteous bumper crop.
Oh, joy when I smell the fresh earthy
scent of rain on a hot summer day

I think of myself as self-sufficient,
hard-working, and resilient,
and perhaps this comes from
parents and grandparents who
instilled these deep-seated values
and character traits in me.

While I apply this tenacity and
hard work in everything that I do,
in my heart of hearts, I wonder
if I was always meant to be
a wild child of the frontier?

Lazy Daisy Days

Lazy Daisy Days

I love my lazy daisy days
carefree and reminiscent
of long-gone childhood

racing bicycles everywhere
doodling with sidewalk chalk
and imagining those days will

last forever or until that old
cowbell brings us home
for hearty family suppers

Are these days gone forever
reserved for happy children
perhaps just memories in slant

of blissful blistering summers
and yet the sweet flowers
or the sound of happy birds

bring it swirling back
in one eternal round
on these lazy daisy days

My Dear Children

I am writing this letter to you as my end is near.
I want to share my love and hope with you.
I recognize that I am not the perfect mother.
I acknowledge the storms that have raged
and the tumult that comes when I struggled
from my core. I did all within my power
to bring back both warmth and peace,
blessing you with the beauty that cycled
through our beautiful warm days
and even our coldest nights.

I fought for you against forces that
have been levied fiercely against me.
Nothing could be done to stop the march
forward as man and industry charged ahead.
I have tried to protect to you.
I desperately wanted the songbirds
to sing the sweetest message of love and hope.

Instead, you are greeted by screeching horns
and growling rumbling raucous engines.
I've tried to provide you with food
carefully grown by gentle hands.
Regrettably, the machines of agribusiness dominate.
My gentle stewards cannot compete against
the quest to make money and more money.

My very lifeblood is now tainted
with micro-plastics and garbage to
further contaminate and destroy me.
I can no longer protect you, my darlings,
and I fear that my time is near.

Forgive me, my dearest children.
I tried to give you all I have, and I failed!
I wished to endure for generations but my end is near.
Again – please accept this letter as a call to action.
Perhaps you can do better. My life is in your hands.

Love, Mother Earth

Get Back Up

Adversity comes in so many ways
and we feel like it's never going to end ~
Recognize it, breathe it, feel it,
Let it be an affirmation of our shared humanity
because none of us are insulated from challenge.

Once we understand that it is through adversity
that we grow, we can begin to chart a new path,
a direction perhaps we have never considered.
That's when we get back up, stand tall and
start again, because we can't quit on ourselves.

Choose to Remember

Do you ever smile at yourself
when you catch your reflection
and see someone you love
in a mirror or window?

Have you said something
and heard voices of a
trusted friend or mentor like
a resonant and tender echo?

Perhaps you've glanced
at your hands only to be
transported back to childhood
with grandma's hands in yours?

Have you caught the smell
of cookies or warm bread
and sighed remembering
a childhood of long ago?

Maybe you should stop to consider that
your life is circular rather than linear
and nothing is ever gone
if you choose to remember

Embrace the Onlyness

You are certainly more
than the harsh labels
that others impose on you.
Your stories and experiences
make you profoundly unique.
To resort to branding
with rash stereotypes
and false assumptions
is my moral failure
not yours.

Perhaps I should intentionally
embrace your onlyness,
learn about what
makes you special,
and what creativity

and exceptional talents
you bring to the workplace
and to the classroom.
Every day I should
pick a new person ~ just one.

Explore their onlyness.
and take the time to
teach and learn and love,
because none of us
are insulated from the
judgments levied against us.
The power is within us, however
to receive and open ourselves
to the amazing revelation
of onlyness in others.

Beginnings and Endings

You've told me, my friend, where the sidewalk ends
and the gap where the street begins.
Songs of innocence echoing and trusting we know
that we walk with the walk that is measured and slow.
Lightened and brightened in hope we shall go.
Refreshed by the peppermint wind.

But life has a way of changing the course,
and it's off the path we tread.
The songs of experience prompt us boldly to go.
Now we run with the run that will help us grow,
and trusting still until we know.
Encouraged by the peppermint wind.

Now at the fork, the less travelled by
Looking beyond to the yellow wood.
Innocence and experience hum in unity's glow
and in stride we strive to keep up with the flow,
for wisdom has come with time to show.
Guided by the peppermint wind.

For beginnings and endings now swirl through
the memories like leaves at our feet.
Please kiss my cheek and let me go.
Alone I walk with a walk that is measured and slow
and I stop as the woods fill up with snow.
Finally, rested by the peppermint wind.

(Inspired by Shel Silverstein, William Blake,
and Robert Frost)

Love in an Armchair

Tucked into the armchair,
I snuggled close to daddy.
He always smelled of hard work
and wood shavings.

I remember his cheeks were rough
from the wind, and his hands
were ragged and gnarled by work,
yet his touch was tender and soft.

My dad built homes,
but he also built children.
Our routine was to read together
every chance we could get.

I remember he held me close and read
favorite stories that never grow old.
He created all the mythical voices
and brought characters to life.

Daddy was my first teacher
of languages, books, and dreams.
Last night I heard my father's voice
as I read my own angel child to sleep.

For the Children

Celebrated and rightfully **blessed**
will be the Earth when it **is**
loved, cherished, and cared for by **a**
gentle steward of the future ~ a **man**
willing to scatter tiny seeds and **who**
understands the vitality of nature and **plants**.
Choosing to tend to slender saplings and **trees**
urging them to grow strong and sturdy **under**
his watchful and careful eye. **Whose**
tireless labor will provide welcomed **shade**
for the children. Something of which **he**
will never enjoy, and yet his determination **will**
restore the Earth to her beauty and bounty. **Never**
will he throw up his hands and choose instead to **sit**.

"Blessed is a man who plants trees under whose shade he
will never sit." Indian proverb

Tears of Heaven

Caress our faces with gentle rain,
Ease the fear hidden deep in our hearts,
Give us peace in this tired world, and
Wash us Lord, in the tears of Heaven.

Bathe us in assurance of a greater good,
Show but a single star among the clouds,
Replace bitterness with tenderness, and
Caress our faces with gentle rain.

Release us of fears beyond our control,
Purify our hearts with the power of rain,
Grant a moment of calm tranquility, and
Ease the fear hidden deep in our hearts.

Restore for a moment the memories,
Splashes and mud-puddle tromps,
Catch raindrops and taste the sky, and
Give us peace in this tired world.

Open wide the windows of our minds,
Receive our humble petitions for grace,
Cleanse the deep recesses of our souls, and
Wash us Lord, in the tears of Heaven.

Tiny Bird in Yonder Tree

Tiny bird in yonder tree
I see you – do you see me?

Other birds are gathered too
Glistening with a touch of dew

Slowly winter chills dispel
"Chirrup" you call, for all is well

Tiny bird – sweet hope you bring
Thank you for the songs you sing

May your day be bright and sweet
Finding worms and seeds to eat

I'll think of you throughout the day
May Gaia's blessings come your way.

Tiny bird in yonder tree
I see you – do you see me?

Into the Music

Into the music I go,
to lose my mind,
and find my soul.

Let me embrace
the melodies I meet
in sweet harmony

Soar in ethereal sounds
Tempestuous rise and fall
In a call of sheer joy

A community strong
Beautifully bound
In the sound of music

Heartbeats in rhythm
a symphony of peace
sweet release of love

Into the music I go,
to lose my mind,
and find my soul.

Season Follows Season

Am I a daylily, Lord?
Is my influence in this
world short-lived?

No, child, your roots run deep,
and as season follows season,
you will continue to bloom.

If you could see the whole garden
you would understand, but for now,
believe me when I say,

"Take therefore no thought for the morrow:
for the morrow shall take thought
for the things of itself."

~Thank you, Lord.